COOL CAREERS

Movie Director

BY AMY RECHNER

BELLWETHER MEDIA • MINNEAPOLIS, MN

Are you ready to take it to the extreme? Torque books thrust you into the action-packed world of sports, vehicles, mystery, and adventure. These books may include dirt, smoke, fire, and dangerous stunts. **WARNING**: read at your own risk.

This edition first published in 2020 by Bellwether Media, Inc.

No part of this publication may be reproduced in whole or in part without written permission of the publisher. For information regarding permission, write to Bellwether Media, Inc., Attention: Permissions Department, 6012 Blue Circle Drive, Minnetonka, MN 55343.

Library of Congress Cataloging-in-Publication Data

Names: Rechner, Amy, author.
Title: Movie Director / by Amy Rechner.
Description: Minneapolis, MN : Bellwether Media, Inc., [2020] | Series:
    Torque : Cool Careers | Audience: Age 7-12. | Audience: Grades 3-7. |
    Includes bibliographical references and index.
Identifiers: LCCN 2018061463 (print) | LCCN 2019004338 (ebook) | ISBN
    9781618916303 (ebook) | ISBN 9781644870631 (hardcover : alk. paper)
Subjects: LCSH: Motion pictures–Production and direction–Vocational
    guidance–Juvenile literature. | Motion picture producers and
    directors–Juvenile literature.
Classification: LCC PN1995.9.P7 (ebook) | LCC PN1995.9.P7 R3765 2020 (print)
    | DDC 791.4302/33–dc23
LC record available at https://lccn.loc.gov/2018061463

Editor: Kate Moening   Designer: Josh Brink

Printed in the United States of America, North Mankato, MN.

TABLE OF CONTENTS

All in a Day's Work

The movie director watches a knight riding a horse. He is shooting an exciting scene. The director films from different angles. The knight rides, then stands still for the camera.

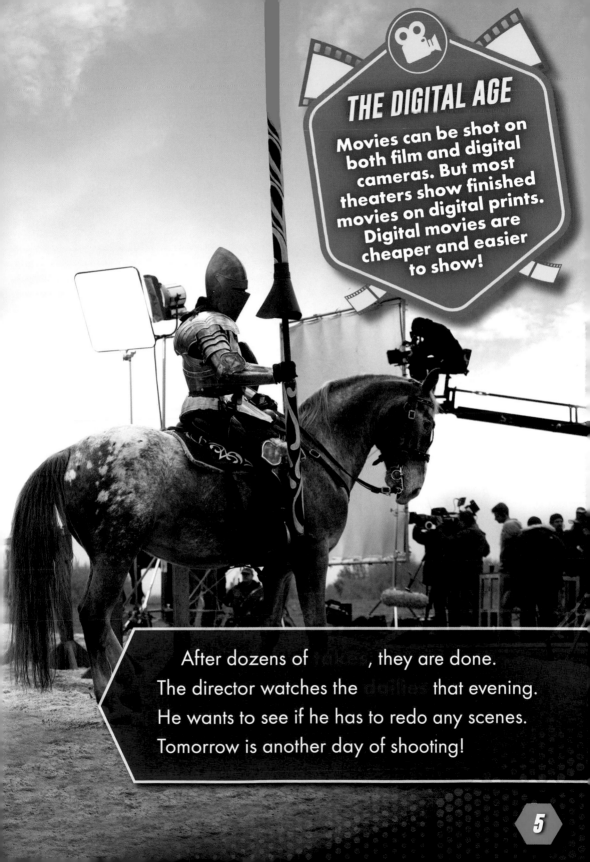

THE DIGITAL AGE

Movies can be shot on both film and digital cameras. But most theaters show finished movies on digital prints. Digital movies are cheaper and easier to show!

After dozens of takes, they are done.
The director watches the dailies that evening.
He wants to see if he has to redo any scenes.
Tomorrow is another day of shooting!

Storytellers in Action

Movie directors are storytellers. They turn words on a page into action on a screen! Directors get many ideas for movies from books or treatments.

Not all movies show in theaters. Many directors make movies for businesses, schools, and television!

Famous Face

Patty Jenkins

BORN:	JULY 24, 1971
HOMETOWN:	LAWRENCE, KANSAS
EDUCATION:	• FINE ARTS DEGREE (THE COOPER UNION)
	• DIRECTING CLASSES (AMERICAN FILM INSTITUTE)
PREVIOUS EXPERIENCE:	• ASSISTANT CAMERA PERSON FOR COMMERCIALS AND MUSIC VIDEOS
	• DIRECTOR OF SEVERAL TV SHOWS AND AWARD-WINNING MOVIES
ACHIEVEMENTS:	• WINNER AND NOMINEE OF MANY FILMMAKING AWARDS
	• WRITER AND PRODUCER FOR MULTIPLE FILMS AND TELEVISION SERIES

CARTOON MOVIE MAGIC

Directors of cartoon movies are a lot like live action directors. They pick the voice actors. They decide how characters look and sound. Then they work with artists to draw their ideas!

Directors make all the important choices for a movie. They choose actors. They hire people to make sets and costumes. They even work with musicians to write music!

Directors put together a production crew to oversee jobs like lighting and sound. They choose a camera director to lead the camera crew. There might be hundreds of people on a crew! All these people allow directors to focus on storytelling.

production crew

Stages of a Story

Some directors have story ideas or scripts brought to them. Other directors find their own stories to tell. They write their own treatments to show to producers.

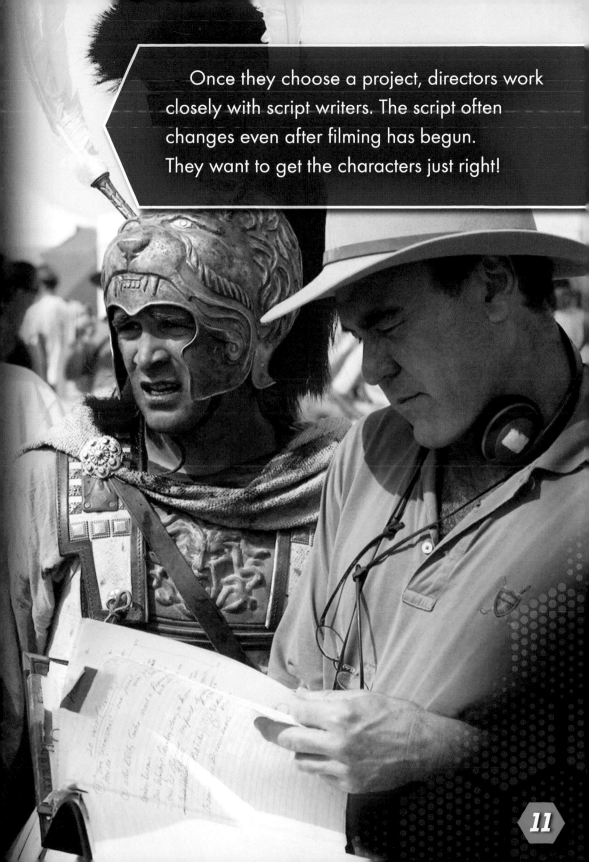

Once they choose a project, directors work closely with script writers. The script often changes even after filming has begun. They want to get the characters just right!

Directors use storyboards to show how the movie will look. Storyboards lay out the movie. They show pictures of each shot. Short notes describe the action in each picture.

Storyboards help directors prepare their shooting schedule. They also help directors share their ideas with their team!

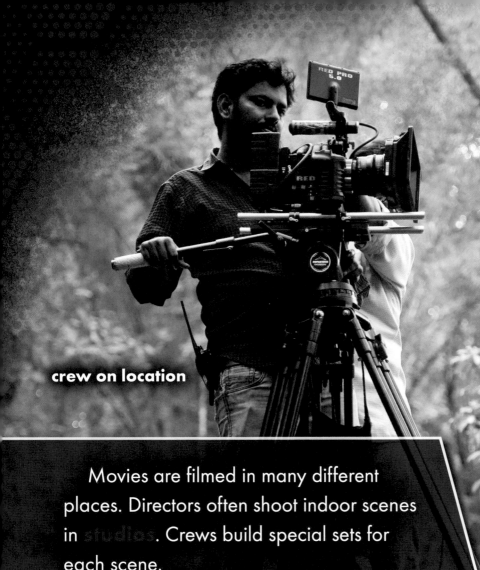

crew on location

Movies are filmed in many different places. Directors often shoot indoor scenes in studios. Crews build special sets for each scene.

Outdoor scenes are often filmed on location. Directors find a place that already looks like the scene they want to film. The actors and production crew live on location for weeks or months.

Shooting Day Checklist

- [x] **5:00 AM: WAKE UP!**

- [x] **6:30 AM: MEET WITH ASSISTANT DIRECTORS ABOUT THE DAY'S SCHEDULE**

- [x] **7:15 AM: MEET WITH CAMERA CREW LEADER ABOUT STORYBOARD AND SHOTS**

- [x] **8:00 AM: BEGIN FILMING!**

- [x] **2:00 PM: LUNCH**

- [x] **8:30 PM: WRAP UP**

- [x] **9:30 PM: REVIEW DAILIES TO SEE IF ANYTHING NEEDS TO BE RESHOT**

- [x] **12:00 AM: BEDTIME!**

After filming, directors start editing.
They take all of the footage and turn it
into a movie. Professional editors help
put the film together in exactly the
right way. Special effects and music
are also added.

SPECIAL EFFECTS

Special effects are part of every movie. Directors use them to make scenes more exciting. They can also fill in details. Even a movie's weather can be a special effect!

The editing room is where directors' ideas really come together. It can take many months or longer to edit a movie.

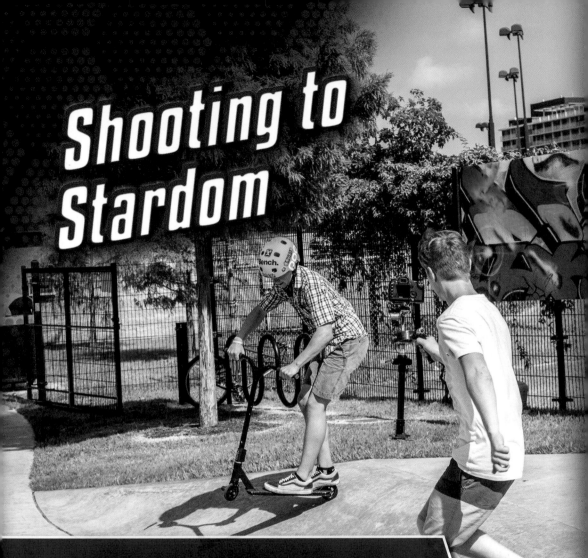

Shooting to Stardom

There are many ways to start learning to direct! Kids can film movies on smartphones or tablets. Parents can help them choose free movie-making apps.

Most people who want a career in film go to college. Many colleges offer classes in film, photography, and the arts.

Career Path

HOBBY MOVIEMAKING

CLASSES AND COLLEGE

JOBS IN FILM, THEATER, OR OTHER ARTS

CREATE A SHOW REEL

DIRECT A MOVIE!

Hopeful directors should work on as many movie sets as they can. They might find work as camera operators or assistant directors. They may get directing work on television commercials or short business videos. Then they can put together a show reel!

Not all movie directors make blockbuster hits. But they all do what they love. They tell stories on film!

Movie Director Wanted!

LOOKING FOR A CREATIVE GENIUS TO DIRECT THE NEXT GREAT FILM! NO LIMITS ON TYPE OF FILM OR STORY.

EDUCATION:	HIGH SCHOOL DIPLOMA; COLLEGE DEGREE IN FILM STUDIES OR RELATED AREA
EXPERIENCE:	FILMS ON SMARTPHONE OR TABLET; JOBS IN MOVIE/TV PRODUCTION; PHOTOGRAPHY AND WRITING EXPERIENCE A PLUS
QUALITIES:	• CREATIVE • ORGANIZED • PATIENT • GOOD WITH PEOPLE

SALARIES FOR THIS POSITION CAN REACH MORE THAN $10 MILLION PER MOVIE!

Glossary

career—a job someone does for a long time

dailies—unedited film shot during one day

editing—putting together by cutting and rearranging

footage—film that has been shot

location—a place outside a movie studio where a movie is shot

producers—people who provide money to have a movie made

production crew—people whose job is to keep movie sets and equipment running smoothly

professional—a person who makes money doing a job

scripts—written forms of movies that show how each scene should be acted and filmed

sets—the backgrounds or rooms that are built for a movie

shooting—the act of photographing or filming

show reel—a collection of clips showing the director's work; directors use show reels to get hired for more work.

studios—spaces that movie companies own that can be used for background in films

takes—scenes that are filmed at one time without stopping

treatments—written pieces of work that summarize a film's story; a treatment is less detailed than a script.

To Learn More

AT THE LIBRARY

Bell, Samantha. *You Can Work in Movies*. North Mankato, Minn.: Capstone Publishing, 2019.

Felix, Rebecca. *Steven Spielberg: Director and Producer of the Jurassic Park Series*. Mankato, Minn.: Abdo Publishing, 2017.

Grabham, Tim. *Video Ideas*. New York, N.Y.: DK Publishing, 2018.

ON THE WEB

FACTSURFER

Factsurfer.com gives you a safe, fun way to find more information.

1. Go to www.factsurfer.com.

2. Enter "movie director" into the search box and click 🔍.

3. Select your book cover to see a list of related web sites.

Index

The images in this book are reproduced through the courtesy of: AF Archive/ Alamy, front cover (hero); fabiodevilla (film crew); Vladimir Wrangel, pp. 4, 5; TCD/ Prod.DB Alamy, pp. 6, 9, 20; Warner Bros/ PhotoFestNYC, p. 7; PictureLux/ Alamy, p. 8; Doane Gregory/ PhotoFestNYC, p. 10; Jaap Buitendijk/ PhotoFestNYC, p. 11; ZUMA Press, Inc./ Alamy, p. 12; RBM Vintage Images/ Alamy, p. 13; pream kumar/ Alamy, p. 14; antb, p. 15 (top); guroXOX, p. 15 (top middle, bottom middle); FraneStockFootages, p. 15 (bottom); Guido Koppes/ Alamy, p. 16; Universal Pictures/ PhotoFestNYC, p. 17; Meinzahn, p. 18; ferrantraite, p. 19 (top left); johnnyslav, p. 19 (top right); gnepphoto, p. 19 (middle left); Gorodenkoff, p. 19 (middle right); ChameleonsEye, p. 19 (bottom); Everett Collection, Inc./ Alamy, p. 21.